Savvy Spender

A Bill Paying Desk Organizer

I0110501

Activinotes

Activinotes

DAILY JOURNALS, PLANNERS, NOTEBOOKS AND OTHER BLANK BOOKS

Personal Information

Last name: Birthdate:

First name: Gender:

Preferred name: Occupation:

Address:

Contact Number:

Email:

Postal Address:

(*If Any*)

Spouse:

Contact Number:

Email:

Mother's Name:

Contact Number:

Email:

Father's Name:

Contact Number:

Email:

Additional Information:

Date: _____

Priority Bills	Amount	Due	Balance	Paid

Other Personal Bills	Amount	Due	Balance	Paid
Total Amount:				

⟡ Notes ⟡

Date: _____

Priority Bills	Amount	Due	Balance	Paid

Other Personal Bills	Amount	Due	Balance	Paid
Total Amount:				

❧ Notes ❧

Date: _____

Priority Bills	Amount	Due	Balance	Paid

Other Personal Bills	Amount	Due	Balance	Paid
Total Amount:				

❧ Notes ❧

Date:_____

Priority Bills	Amount	Due	Balance	Paid

Other Personal Bills	Amount	Due	Balance	Paid
Total Amount:				

❧ Notes ❧

Date:_____

Priority Bills	Amount	Due	Balance	Paid

Other Personal Bills	Amount	Due	Balance	Paid
Total Amount:				

⊷⊷ Notes ⊷⊷

Date:_____

Priority Bills	Amount	Due	Balance	Paid

Other Personal Bills	Amount	Due	Balance	Paid
Total Amount:				

⸻ Notes ⸻

Date: _____

Priority Bills	Amount	Due	Balance	Paid

Other Personal Bills	Amount	Due	Balance	Paid
Total Amount:				

—❦— Notes —❦—

My Spending Chart

		1	2	3	4	5	6	7
	10							
	9							
	8							
	7							
	6							
	5							
	4							
	3							
	2							
	1							
		1	2	3	4	5	6	7

- _____
- _____
- _____
- _____

Date:_____

Priority Bills	Amount	Due	Balance	Paid

Other Personal Bills	Amount	Due	Balance	Paid
Total Amount:				

—❧ Notes ❧—

Date:_____

Priority Bills	Amount	Due	Balance	Paid
Other Personal Bills	**Amount**	**Due**	**Balance**	**Paid**
Total Amount:				

Notes

Date: _____

Priority Bills	Amount	Due	Balance	Paid

Other Personal Bills	Amount	Due	Balance	Paid
Total Amount:				

— Notes —

Date: _____

Priority Bills	Amount	Due	Balance	Paid
Other Personal Bills	Amount	Due	Balance	Paid
Total Amount:				

⋙ Notes ⋘

Date: _____

Priority Bills	Amount	Due	Balance	Paid

Other Personal Bills	Amount	Due	Balance	Paid
Total Amount:				

⚬ Notes ⚬

Date:_____

Priority Bills	Amount	Due	Balance	Paid
Other Personal Bills	Amount	Due	Balance	Paid
Total Amount:				

⊷⊶ Notes ⊷⊶

Date:_____

Priority Bills	Amount	Due	Balance	Paid

Other Personal Bills	Amount	Due	Balance	Paid
Total Amount:				

—◦◦❖ Notes ❖◦◦—

My Spending Chart

	10							
	9							
	8							
	7							
	6							
	5							
	4							
	3							
	2							
	1							
		1	2	3	4	5	6	7

- _____
- _____
- _____
- _____

Date: _____

Priority Bills	Amount	Due	Balance	Paid

Other Personal Bills	Amount	Due	Balance	Paid
Total Amount:				

❧ Notes ❧

Savvy Spender—A Bill Paying Desk Organizer

Date:

Priority Bills	Amount	Due	Balance	Paid

Other Personal Bills	Amount	Due	Balance	Paid
Total Amount:				

—◦◦◦ Notes ◦◦◦—

Date: _____

Priority Bills	Amount	Due	Balance	Paid

Other Personal Bills	Amount	Due	Balance	Paid
Total Amount:				

— Notes —

Savvy Spender—A Bill Paying Desk Organizer

Date:_____

Priority Bills	Amount	Due	Balance	Paid

Other Personal Bills	Amount	Due	Balance	Paid
Total Amount:				

❧ Notes ❧

23

Savvy Spender—A Bill Paying Desk Organizer

Date: _____

Priority Bills	Amount	Due	Balance	Paid

Other Personal Bills	Amount	Due	Balance	Paid
Total Amount:				

Notes

Date:_____

Priority Bills	Amount	Due	Balance	Paid

Other Personal Bills	Amount	Due	Balance	Paid
Total Amount:				

⋙⋘ Notes ⋙⋘

Date: _____

Priority Bills	Amount	Due	Balance	Paid

Other Personal Bills	Amount	Due	Balance	Paid
Total Amount:				

—◆— Notes —◆—

My Spending Chart

		1	2	3	4	5	6	7
	10							
	9							
	8							
	7							
	6							
	5							
	4							
	3							
	2							
	1							
		1	2	3	4	5	6	7

- _____
- _____
- _____
- _____

Date: _____

Priority Bills	Amount	Due	Balance	Paid

Other Personal Bills	Amount	Due	Balance	Paid
Total Amount:				

—◆— Notes —◆—

Date:_____

Priority Bills	Amount	Due	Balance	Paid

Other Personal Bills	Amount	Due	Balance	Paid
Total Amount:				

❧ Notes ❧

Date: _____

Priority Bills	Amount	Due	Balance	Paid
Other Personal Bills	Amount	Due	Balance	Paid
Total Amount:				

❖ Notes ❖

Date: _____

Priority Bills	Amount	Due	Balance	Paid

Other Personal Bills	Amount	Due	Balance	Paid
Total Amount:				

—◆— Notes —◆—

Date: _____

Priority Bills	Amount	Due	Balance	Paid

Other Personal Bills	Amount	Due	Balance	Paid
Total Amount:				

❧ Notes ❧

Date: _____

Priority Bills	Amount	Due	Balance	Paid

Other Personal Bills	Amount	Due	Balance	Paid
Total Amount:				

❦ Notes ❦

Date: _____

Priority Bills	Amount	Due	Balance	Paid

Other Personal Bills	Amount	Due	Balance	Paid
Total Amount:				

—◆— Notes —◆—

My Spending Chart

		1	2	3	4	5	6	7
	10							
	9							
	8							
	7							
	6							
	5							
	4							
	3							
	2							
	1							
		1	2	3	4	5	6	7

- _____
- _____
- _____
- _____

Date:_____

Priority Bills	Amount	Due	Balance	Paid

Other Personal Bills	Amount	Due	Balance	Paid
Total Amount:				

⋙⋘ Notes ⋙⋘

Date: _____

Priority Bills	Amount	Due	Balance	Paid
Other Personal Bills	**Amount**	**Due**	**Balance**	**Paid**
Total Amount:				

Notes

Date: _____

Priority Bills	Amount	Due	Balance	Paid

Other Personal Bills	Amount	Due	Balance	Paid
Total Amount:				

--- Notes ---

Date: ____________________

Priority Bills	Amount	Due	Balance	Paid

Other Personal Bills	Amount	Due	Balance	Paid
Total Amount:				

Notes

Date: _____

Priority Bills	Amount	Due	Balance	Paid
Other Personal Bills	Amount	Due	Balance	Paid
Total Amount:				

❧ Notes ❧

Date: _____

Priority Bills	Amount	Due	Balance	Paid
Other Personal Bills	**Amount**	**Due**	**Balance**	**Paid**
Total Amount:				

------ Notes ------

Date: _____

Priority Bills	Amount	Due	Balance	Paid

Other Personal Bills	Amount	Due	Balance	Paid
Total Amount:				

—◊— Notes —◊—

My Spending Chart

	10							
	9							
	8							
	7							
	6							
	5							
	4							
	3							
	2							
	1							
		1	2	3	4	5	6	7

- _____

- _____

- _____

- _____

Date:_____

Priority Bills	Amount	Due	Balance	Paid

Other Personal Bills	Amount	Due	Balance	Paid
Total Amount:				

⋙ Notes ⋘

Date:_____

Priority Bills	Amount	Due	Balance	Paid

Other Personal Bills	Amount	Due	Balance	Paid
Total Amount:				

——◇— Notes —◇——

Date: _____

Priority Bills	Amount	Due	Balance	Paid

Other Personal Bills	Amount	Due	Balance	Paid
Total Amount:				

⟨Notes⟩

Date: _____

Priority Bills	Amount	Due	Balance	Paid

Other Personal Bills	Amount	Due	Balance	Paid
Total Amount:				

⋙ Notes ⋘

Date: ____________________

Priority Bills	Amount	Due	Balance	Paid
Other Personal Bills	**Amount**	**Due**	**Balance**	**Paid**
Total Amount:				

Notes

Date: _____

Priority Bills	Amount	Due	Balance	Paid

Other Personal Bills	Amount	Due	Balance	Paid
Total Amount:				

❧ Notes ❧

Date: _____

Priority Bills	Amount	Due	Balance	Paid

Other Personal Bills	Amount	Due	Balance	Paid
Total Amount:				

—≪≫— Notes —≪≫—

My Spending Chart

		1	2	3	4	5	6	7
	10							
	9							
	8							
	7							
	6							
	5							
	4							
	3							
	2							
	1							
		1	2	3	4	5	6	7

- _____
- _____
- _____
- _____

Date: _____

Priority Bills	Amount	Due	Balance	Paid

Other Personal Bills	Amount	Due	Balance	Paid
Total Amount:				

⟶⟨⟩ Notes ⟨⟩⟵

Date: _____

Priority Bills	Amount	Due	Balance	Paid

Other Personal Bills	Amount	Due	Balance	Paid
Total Amount:				

Notes

Date: _____

Priority Bills	Amount	Due	Balance	Paid

Other Personal Bills	Amount	Due	Balance	Paid
Total Amount:				

❧ Notes ❧

Date: _____

Priority Bills	Amount	Due	Balance	Paid
Other Personal Bills	Amount	Due	Balance	Paid
Total Amount:				

Notes

Date:_____

Priority Bills	Amount	Due	Balance	Paid

Other Personal Bills	Amount	Due	Balance	Paid
Total Amount:				

— Notes —

Date: _____

Priority Bills	Amount	Due	Balance	Paid

Other Personal Bills	Amount	Due	Balance	Paid
Total Amount:				

—≪≫— Notes —≪≫—

Date: _____

Priority Bills	Amount	Due	Balance	Paid

Other Personal Bills	Amount	Due	Balance	Paid
Total Amount:				

⊷⊷⊷ Notes ⊷⊷⊷

My Spending Chart

	10							
	9							
	8							
	7							
	6							
	5							
	4							
	3							
	2							
	1							
		1	2	3	4	5	6	7

- _____
- _____
- _____
- _____

Date: _____

Priority Bills	Amount	Due	Balance	Paid
Other Personal Bills	Amount	Due	Balance	Paid
Total Amount:				

━◅◇▻━ Notes ━◅◇▻━

Savvy Spender—A Bill Paying Desk Organizer

Date: _____

Priority Bills	Amount	Due	Balance	Paid

Other Personal Bills	Amount	Due	Balance	Paid
Total Amount:				

Notes

Date: _____

Priority Bills	Amount	Due	Balance	Paid

Other Personal Bills	Amount	Due	Balance	Paid
Total Amount:				

—◦◦◦— Notes —◦◦◦—

Date: _____

Priority Bills	Amount	Due	Balance	Paid

Other Personal Bills	Amount	Due	Balance	Paid
Total Amount:				

❧ Notes ❧

Date:_____

Priority Bills	Amount	Due	Balance	Paid

Other Personal Bills	Amount	Due	Balance	Paid
Total Amount:				

—◆— Notes —◆—

Date: _____

Priority Bills	Amount	Due	Balance	Paid

Other Personal Bills	Amount	Due	Balance	Paid
Total Amount:				

⟨⟩ Notes ⟨⟩

Date: _____

Priority Bills	Amount	Due	Balance	Paid
Other Personal Bills	Amount	Due	Balance	Paid
Total Amount:				

◄◇► Notes ◄◇►

My Spending Chart

		1	2	3	4	5	6	7
	10							
	9							
	8							
	7							
	6							
	5							
	4							
	3							
	2							
	1							
		1	2	3	4	5	6	7

- _____
- _____
- _____
- _____

Date: _____

Priority Bills	Amount	Due	Balance	Paid

Other Personal Bills	Amount	Due	Balance	Paid
Total Amount:				

❧❦ Notes ❦❧

Date:_____

Priority Bills	Amount	Due	Balance	Paid

Other Personal Bills	Amount	Due	Balance	Paid
Total Amount:				

⟞⊸ Notes ⊷⟝

Date: _____

Priority Bills	Amount	Due	Balance	Paid

Other Personal Bills	Amount	Due	Balance	Paid
Total Amount:				

— Notes —

Date:_____

Priority Bills	Amount	Due	Balance	Paid

Other Personal Bills	Amount	Due	Balance	Paid
Total Amount:				

—◆— Notes —◆—

Date:_____

Priority Bills	Amount	Due	Balance	Paid
Other Personal Bills	**Amount**	**Due**	**Balance**	**Paid**
Total Amount:				

—⊷ Notes ⊶—

Date: _____

Priority Bills	Amount	Due	Balance	Paid

Other Personal Bills	Amount	Due	Balance	Paid
Total Amount:				

⟶⟨⟩ Notes ⟨⟩⟵

Date: _____

Priority Bills	Amount	Due	Balance	Paid

Other Personal Bills	Amount	Due	Balance	Paid
Total Amount:				

— Notes —

My Spending Chart

	10							
	9							
	8							
	7							
	6							
	5							
	4							
	3							
	2							
	1							
		1	2	3	4	5	6	7

- _____
- _____
- _____
- _____

Date:_____

Priority Bills	Amount	Due	Balance	Paid

Other Personal Bills	Amount	Due	Balance	Paid
Total Amount:				

--- ◦◦◦ Notes ◦◦◦ ---

Date: _____

Priority Bills	Amount	Due	Balance	Paid

Other Personal Bills	Amount	Due	Balance	Paid
Total Amount:				

Notes

Date: _____

Priority Bills	Amount	Due	Balance	Paid

Other Personal Bills	Amount	Due	Balance	Paid
Total Amount:				

❧ Notes ❧

Date:_____

Priority Bills	Amount	Due	Balance	Paid

Other Personal Bills	Amount	Due	Balance	Paid
Total Amount:				

⋘ Notes ⋙

Date:_____

Priority Bills	Amount	Due	Balance	Paid

Other Personal Bills	Amount	Due	Balance	Paid
Total Amount:				

⊸⊷ Notes ⊶⊷

Date: _____

Priority Bills	Amount	Due	Balance	Paid

Other Personal Bills	Amount	Due	Balance	Paid
Total Amount:				

⟶∞⟶ Notes ⟵∞⟵

Date: _____

Priority Bills	Amount	Due	Balance	Paid

Other Personal Bills	Amount	Due	Balance	Paid
Total Amount:				

Notes

My Spending Chart

		1	2	3	4	5	6	7
	10							
	9							
	8							
	7							
	6							
	5							
	4							
	3							
	2							
	1							
		1	2	3	4	5	6	7

- _____

- _____

- _____

- _____

Date: _____

Priority Bills	Amount	Due	Balance	Paid

Other Personal Bills	Amount	Due	Balance	Paid
Total Amount:				

⟨⟩ Notes ⟨⟩

Savvy Spender—A Bill Paying Desk Organizer

Date:_____

Priority Bills	Amount	Due	Balance	Paid

Other Personal Bills	Amount	Due	Balance	Paid
Total Amount:				

—◆— Notes —◆—

Date: _____

Priority Bills	Amount	Due	Balance	Paid

Other Personal Bills	Amount	Due	Balance	Paid
Total Amount:				

❦ Notes ❦

Date: _____

Priority Bills	Amount	Due	Balance	Paid
Other Personal Bills	**Amount**	**Due**	**Balance**	**Paid**
Total Amount:				

⊷⊷⊷ Notes ⊷⊷⊷

Date: _____

Priority Bills	Amount	Due	Balance	Paid

Other Personal Bills	Amount	Due	Balance	Paid
Total Amount:				

—❦— Notes —❦—

Date: _____

Priority Bills	Amount	Due	Balance	Paid

Other Personal Bills	Amount	Due	Balance	Paid
Total Amount:				

────◄◄►► Notes ◄◄►►────

Date: _____

Priority Bills	Amount	Due	Balance	Paid

Other Personal Bills	Amount	Due	Balance	Paid
Total Amount:				

❧ Notes ❧

My Spending Chart

	10							
	9							
	8							
	7							
	6							
	5							
	4							
	3							
	2							
	1							
		1	2	3	4	5	6	7

- _____
- _____
- _____
- _____

Date:_____

Priority Bills	Amount	Due	Balance	Paid

Other Personal Bills	Amount	Due	Balance	Paid
Total Amount:				

⚬⚬ Notes ⚬⚬

Date: _____

Priority Bills	Amount	Due	Balance	Paid

Other Personal Bills	Amount	Due	Balance	Paid
Total Amount:				

⟶◇⟵ Notes ⟶◇⟵

Date: _____

Priority Bills	Amount	Due	Balance	Paid

Other Personal Bills	Amount	Due	Balance	Paid
Total Amount:				

⋙ Notes ⋘

Date: _____

Priority Bills	Amount	Due	Balance	Paid
Other Personal Bills	**Amount**	**Due**	**Balance**	**Paid**
Total Amount:				

⟨∞⟩ Notes ⟨∞⟩

Date:_____

Priority Bills	Amount	Due	Balance	Paid

Other Personal Bills	Amount	Due	Balance	Paid
Total Amount:				

⟐ Notes ⟐

Date: _____

Priority Bills	Amount	Due	Balance	Paid

Other Personal Bills	Amount	Due	Balance	Paid
Total Amount:				

❋❈❋ Notes ❋❈❋

Date: _____

Priority Bills	Amount	Due	Balance	Paid

Other Personal Bills	Amount	Due	Balance	Paid
Total Amount:				

=•= Notes =•=

My Spending Chart

	10							
	9							
	8							
	7							
	6							
	5							
	4							
	3							
	2							
	1							
		1	2	3	4	5	6	7

- _____
- _____
- _____
- _____

Date:_____

Priority Bills	Amount	Due	Balance	Paid

Other Personal Bills	Amount	Due	Balance	Paid
Total Amount:				

~⋘⋙~ Notes ~⋘⋙~

Date: _____

Priority Bills	Amount	Due	Balance	Paid
Other Personal Bills	**Amount**	**Due**	**Balance**	**Paid**
Total Amount:				

⟞⟋ Notes ⟍⟝

Date: _____

Priority Bills	Amount	Due	Balance	Paid

Other Personal Bills	Amount	Due	Balance	Paid
Total Amount:				

─◅◆▻─ Notes ─◅◆▻─

Date:_____

Priority Bills	Amount	Due	Balance	Paid

Other Personal Bills	Amount	Due	Balance	Paid
Total Amount:				

❧ Notes ❧

Date: _____

Priority Bills	Amount	Due	Balance	Paid

Other Personal Bills	Amount	Due	Balance	Paid
Total Amount:				

∞ Notes ∞

Date: _____

Priority Bills		Amount	Due	Balance	Paid
Other Personal Bills		**Amount**	**Due**	**Balance**	**Paid**
Total Amount:					

❧ Notes ❧

www.ingramcontent.com/pod-product-compliance
Lightning Source LLC
Chambersburg PA
CBHW081336090426
42737CB00017B/3165